PERSUASIVE PUBLIC SPEAKING

Simple steps to win over any audience

Written by Nicolas Martin
Translated by Carly Probert

Coaching 50MINUTES.com

PUBLIC SPEAKING

- **Problem:** How can I manage my nerves and overcome fear in order to successfully speak in public?
- **Uses:** It is impossible to escape public speaking in the professional world. Whatever the form of public speaking, managing stress in order to develop and improve speaking skills in any environment is beneficial to all.
- **Professional context:** Searching for jobs (individual or group interviews), internal presentations (project proposals, service objectives, outcomes, meeting minutes), professional speeches (conferences, seminars, training sessions, fairs, presentations at universities/schools).
- **FAQs:**
  - Why are we afraid of public speaking?
  - What practical exercises can help to overcome stress?
  - How can I prepare my speech?
  - What mistakes should be avoided?
  - What should I do if I lose my train of thought during my presentation?
  - How can I remain calm when faced with a difficult question?
  - Should I be afraid of silence?
  - Is a *PowerPoint* presentation always necessary?

All speeches, whether to large or small audiences, are different, mainly due to the fact that the audience itself is never the same. The subjects also vary and, unless the speaker is an expert in the topic, this can be an additional source of anguish. However, there are also external parameters to consider, such as preparation time, the location of the presentation and personal events, which can all disrupt even the most talented of speakers.

That said, are we condemned to always view public speaking as if it were a laborious task? If even the best speakers cannot control all the parameters that make a public speech successful, what will become of us mere mortals? Are we reduced to always apprehend this type of speaking? Or, worse still, once we have overcome the fear of speaking, are we then left inevitably stuck in a vicious circle that we cannot escape, since it is impossible to completely control the situation?

This certainly seems like a sad fate! However, although it is impossible for us to control everything to avoid stress, it is easy to reduce it substantially using methods and exercises that anyone can do, provided they are prepared to make all the changes necessary to succeed.

As this is a process that occurs throughout life, due to its subjective and evolving nature, it is necessary to carry out this exercise by discovering and personally applying the actionable insights, methods and tips that will make you understand that public speaking does not have to be a torturous affair. In just a short time, you will come to feel excited at the idea of your next public speaking opportunity.

> Ever since my childhood, I have repeatedly found myself in the spotlight: first surrounded by dozens of other people in dance recitals, then I joined a band soon after and sat behind a microphone during various concerts. Although it was

there, my stress never seemed to paralyse me.

Despite relatively frequent exposure to the public, the idea of speaking in front of a group still proved difficult and perilous. There would be a knot in my stomach leading up to the moment (sometimes for up to an hour), and then, from my very first sentence, my cheeks would flush red, closely followed by the rest of my face. It was impossible to hide the redness! Besides making me feel completely ridiculous, this disrupted my concentration and made the exercise impossible. Being someone who is not normally shy, I cannot understand why I got into such a state.

It was ultimately through music that I found my answer: in reality, what frightened me was improvisation. In the same way that I was unable to think up lyrics for a musical battle, I found it really difficult to answer questions during presentations that were unexpected, or generally outside of the framework that I had set for the speech.

The stress linked to the difficulty of improvising when faced with an immediate unanticipated reaction is still an obstacle which I experience as part of my professional life. As a broadcast manager for an artistic company, my main role is to call the programmers who are approached dozens of times a day and convince them to broadcast many of my shows. Being able to perfectly present a show (that I sometimes had not seen) and respond to any potential qualms or objections was not yet a part of my job that I could control completely.

However, as speaking was an integral part of my studies, and now also of my professional life, I learned to get around this, instead of try to resolve it.

Testimony by Anne Rouchouse (broadcasting manager in the cultural sector)

THE KEY TO BECOMING A CONFIDENT SPEAKER

We don't need to look at specific numbers to realise that a significant number of people suffer from this phobia. The fear of public speaking, or "glossophobia" – from the Greek 'glossa' meaning "language" and 'phobos' meaning "fear" – is one of the most commonly shared fears. In fact, at least three out of four people feel anxious at the thought of speaking in front of a group. In other words, most of the people sat before you at one of your presentations would also feel stressed if they were in your position. Although this can be reassuring at first, it is unfortunately far from sufficient to help you overcome the "insurmountable".

Overcoming your fear of public speaking and delivering a dynamic and controlled presentation are the results of a long process. You cannot rely solely on your skills, as each presentation is different. However, you can develop a method and tricks, which you can then take ownership of and adapt to suit your presentations, depending on the individual circumstances.

THE PREMISES TO ASK ALL QUESTIONS

Step one: Brainstorming

Brainstorming, or "mind-mapping", is a technique that is frequently used in the professional world, as it presents several undeniable advantages. As part of the preparation for speaking in public, where you are the main speaker, this technique may be useful for listing everything that you don't personally enjoy, as well as everything that captures your attention during a presentation.

This reflection should be done before any other presentation planning; it takes place even before setting goals for what you want the presentation to achieve because once you are immersed in a specific topic, you may no longer be in the mindset that allows you to think of the ideal structure for a persuasive speech, whatever the topic. This technique is not designed to help you to create a structure for a particular presentation topic, but a methodology for all future speaking. The objectives of brainstorming are:

- Firstly, to detach yourself from too rigid a framework and allow yourself to focus your thoughts on items that appear less relevant at first;
- Secondly, to ensure that you are calm in the early stages of the preparation process and get started on the right foot as soon as possible, and thus gradually alleviate your stress and apprehension.

From your observations, you should start to see the structure that your future presentation should take a little more clearly. Also, as a successful presentation strikes a good balance between form and substance, it is possible for you to apply this technique to all topics. You then need to judge its value depending on the knowledge you already have on the subject and what you need to accomplish.

For those who are very anxious, taking the time to also brainstorm for the background is equally important. An overview of your knowledge on the subject from the outset – do I need to do additional research to master the topic? – will, once again, allow you to continue fighting your stress by directly targeting its potential sources. Indeed, during a speech, a lot of stress comes from the fact that we sometimes do not have a strong command of certain areas, and we fear that this will be discovered on the day. We therefore recommend a broad sweep to stay calm!

Step two: Choosing a framework

Before you dive into preparing your speech, it is necessary to ask yourself some preliminary questions.

- **What type of public am I going to be speaking to?** The important point is whether it is a homogenous or heterogeneous public, trained experts or novices, as well as determining their expectations.
- **What is the overall purpose of my speech?** To inform? To train? To convince? To persuade? To entertain?
- **What are the sub-objectives?** You can choose up to three. They are derived from the main objective, but

are more precise, often quantifiable. For example, most people (3/4 of participants) must know how to use the new interface of the intranet after attending the presentation.

- **How can I achieve these goals?** The means can be both tangible and intangible: your expertise, your ability to explain or respond to questions effectively, etc.
- **What are my strengths?** Do not hesitate to coach yourself or highlight your qualities.

EXTRA INFORMATION

Far too many people have a tendency to denigrate and treat public speaking as a punishment, especially if it is imposed upon them. However, reflecting on your own qualities allows you to avoid this defeatist attitude and place yourself on the other side, that of "self-defense" and full awareness of your own capabilities.

Planning a presentation

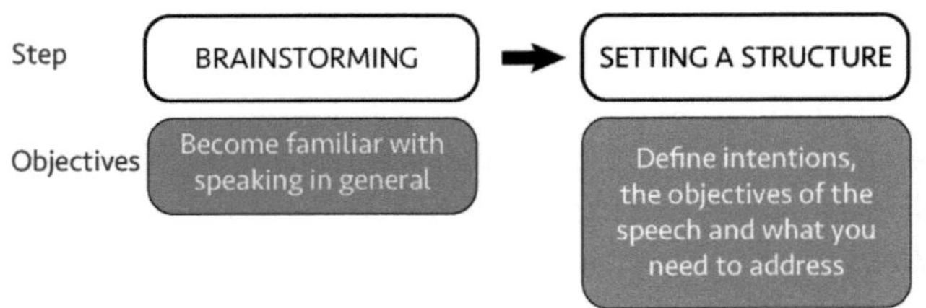

PREPARATION FOR COMPLETE CONTROL OF A PRESENTATION

Preparation should be your top priority. Personal coaches and subject experts will tell you that more than three quarters of your success lies in your ability to prepare yourself. Just like the preliminary questions, you must focus equally on both substance and structure.

Substance

You have already reflected on the content of your speech through the initial brainstorming. Now you can simplify the work by taking into account three key elements:

- Research the information that you do not yet have;
- Arrange ideas by developing a clear plan to deliver a specific, powerful and professional message;
- Drafting some or all of your speech, to serve as a "score" during rehearsals.

> **TOP TIP**
>
> Write your entire speech out to begin. This will allow you to question the ideas you want to develop in your own words, taking ownership of the problem while continuing your fight against stress.

If you intend to rely on a *PowerPoint* presentation on the dreaded day, take this opportunity to start putting it together. However, be careful not to tackle too many steps at once! It is better to start by writing the slides only, with simple text on a white background. You can then focus on the formatting later.

Structure

Once the foundation work is underway, it is time to think of the structure that you will give to your ideas. Take the plan that you made in advance to easily switch between topics for your presentations.

At this stage, you need to return to what you put on paper when brainstorming and adapt it to suit an oral style as, however well-written it may be, it will inevitably appear heavier and less natural when spoken aloud. Therefore, you must work particularly hard on this aspect so as not to risk losing your audience's attention.

ADAPTING YOUR SPEECH

Although using technical jargon may reassure you, do not commit the mistake of believing that your audience will be composed of experts in the field. Therefore, make sure to simplify the subject you are dealing with, even popularising some information if needed.

Use metaphors adapted to your audience as much as possible. If you are responsible for presenting a more complex project or a technical change, don't hesitate to illustrate your points with clear comparisons that speak to all.

This requirement related to language will require you to dedicate time and open your mind. Besides, in principle, researching information and arranging your ideas represents a small amount of your time.

Again, you should work methodically:

- topic after topic, according to the sequence of your presentation;
- according to your media, such as a *PowerPoint* presentation, if you have decided to use one.

Simulation

To better visualise the flow of a more oral style, here is an example of a presentation on recommendations regarding the cultural action of France in the world, in order to regain its dynamism and cultural influence.

- **Written speech:**

> If France wishes to find a cultural radiation that is compa-
> rable to the last century, its external cultural action needs
> to focus on a three-step strategy, which is conducted simul-
> taneously, not separately from each other.
> Indeed, it is necessary for France to, on the one hand, stabi-
> lise its cultural network deployed overseas, but also present
> inside of the country, the reforms in respect to both quality
> and quantity. It is essential to conduct an evaluation of the
> image of cultural action abroad in order to understand the
> different perceptions, not to solve the issues that continue
> to affect the internal network.
> On the other hand, the network must conduct a parallel
> valuation policy on the key action areas by making them a
> priority in certain geographic areas. This is mainly a question
> of cinematographic sectors, musical as well as literary,
> including books and written works.
> Finally, to complete this three-step strategy, France must
> affirm the shift operated in its cultural policy, namely
> intercultural and interdisciplinary dimensions of its action
> abroad. Whether festivals in Latin America, hospitality
> artists and other cultures in the country, the defence of
> cultural factors such as the international heritage of Syria
> and Mali, or the defence of threatened peoples, such as
> the Uighurs. France could position its action in a dynamic
> cultural mutual cooperation and find some global influence.

The three essential elements are visibly distinctly written in the three paragraphs. Now these three paragraphs will need more visibility in an oral style.

- **Oral speech:**

> Three recommendations are to be issued as part of the cultural action outside of France. If the country wants to regain some global cultural influence, French cultural diplomacy must first stabilise (need for stabilisation) in its network, the nature and pace of reforms, the awareness of its current image and the resolution of internal issues. It will then need to upgrade (need for revaluation) some particular policy areas, such as cinema, music, books and writings, and finally assert (need for affirmation) more cultural and interdisciplinary policies (e.g. festival in Latin America + home artists and foreign cultures + defence of cultural causes, such as Syria and Mali + defence of threatened peoples, i.e. Uygur people).

The words used are more generic and the sentence structure is similar, while the use of words such as "need" allows for the highlighting of the three key words that we want the audience to focus on: stabilisation, revaluation and affirmation. The speaking of these three keywords can be accompanied by a gesture that pushes the audience to glance at the *PowerPoint* diagram.

- ***PowerPoint* slide layout**

Example PowerPoint

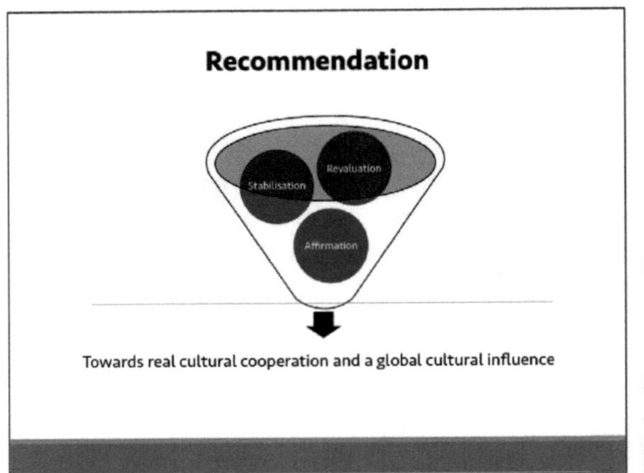

The slide is clean without text overload. Keywords appear separately and are positioned in a diagram for understanding the relationship between ideas. There is no need to include the examples which appear in your speech and explain the keywords.

audience will actively participate in making the effort to understand the links between what they see and the words you say.

Training or repetitions

Now that you have gathered all the items, you can start rehearsing the presentation with more serenity and control. As a period for making adjustments, this time is for matching the content and structure.

Training yourself requires you to let go, because you have to allow things to unfold naturally and logically. The ideas, which you think follow a certain chain of thought, may be clearer if you show them another way. Using your media may also pose questions. Does your *PowerPoint* facilitate the understanding of your speech? Does it make things more complicated than they need to be?

This time, which is closest to the speaking you will be doing, deserves your full attention because it will allow you to adjust many passages of the presentation. You should dedicate enough time to the structure, for the simple reason that this ensures continuity, and practice in front of different audiences so as to cover all eventualities!

- Alone, in order to adjust your speech and your slides, and offer your audience a coherent speech that is accurate and professional.
- In front of one or two people you know, to test your body language, your magnetism and the clarity of your words.

- In front of one or two people that are similar to those who will make up your audience on the day, to test more technical aspects and prepare for other questions which you may not have considered.

With these scenario-based exercises, you will benefit from direct feedback from your "guinea pigs". Now you can rectify and refine some details! Moreover, by rehearsing your presentation differently, you will master the content with little effort and you will have more time to tackle what you fear most: being confronted with the eyes of the audience.

Preparing a presentation

The necessary steps to move forward

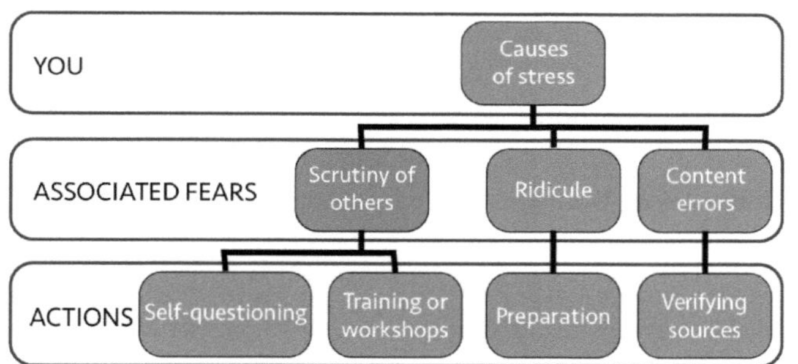

MANAGING THE DEVELOPMENT OF YOUR PRESENTATION

The big day is fast approaching. You took the time to master and understand your subject, your *PowerPoint* presentation, your speech and how to deliver it. Yet, you continue to feel stressed just thinking about the rest of the room. Do not panic and take time to relax using some exercises.

Breathing exercises before your presentation

To reduce your stress before you start, you can perform some simple breathing exercises that will take you a few minutes.

- **Breathing in fours:** Count to four as you breathe in and hold your breath for another four seconds, then exhale for a count of four and hold your breath again for another four seconds. You can repeat this cycle for ten minutes to allow you to regulate your breathing and your heartbeat.
- **Breathing in motion:** Take a little walk and focus on your breathing by inhaling through the nose and exhaling through the mouth as you walk. You can go around the block or the building, depending on your environment.
- **Liberating breathing:** Inhale deeply and exhale while throwing your arms towards the floor at the same time. Projecting your arms towards the floor can be liberating, as though you are throwing away your stress and apprehension towards the ground. Feel free to go somewhere private to carry out this exercise!

Points to keep in mind during your presentation

The presentation begins. You did some exercises, slowed your heart rate and it is now time to begin.

If you have the opportunity, exchange a few words with a person you know before you start your speech. The aim of this is to distract your attention from the impending task, making you think of anything else to avoid cancelling out the effects of the relaxation exercises. Given the preparation you did at the beginning, there is no reason to stress a few minutes before the start!

During your presentation, try as much as you can to:

* note your overall consistency because changes, regardless of their nature, can disrupt the audience and divert their attention from the speech;
* take time to breathe;
* control your rate of speech;
* keep a bottle of water handy;
* not be afraid of silence for a few seconds;
* not remain static;
* remain optimistic and positive.

WHAT TO AVOID

Avoid escaping the gaze of the audience or staring into space. Everyone has tried these techniques and they only draw attention to your anxiety. Instead, try to interest yourself in your audience, for example by asking for the list of participants in advance or learning the profile of some people present at your speech.

Contingencies to work on yourself

If, during the preparation phase, contingencies were already stressful, by anticipating early questions, reactions or hazards, you will feel the same during the presentation. Some, having mastered the finer points of their presentation, will not feel overwhelmed by an unexpected issue or remark, while others may lose their train of thought entirely. If you belong to the second group, you know that learning to better respond to unforeseen events is a long process and that will not change in one presentation. It is precisely by doing them that you can apply some techniques and better manage these unexpected interruptions.

In general, by initiating introspection on yourself to better respond to the unexpected, you will learn to:

- manage your emotions and therefore know yourself better;
- become adaptable and flexible;
- gain perspective and remain optimistic.

Although all advance preparation for a public speech is a good thing, it can also make you closed to the unexpected and therefore less natural and open to discussion. That is why it is best to keep in mind from the beginning that you cannot control certain things, and to use this gained time to work more on managing your reactions in unexpected situations. You will gain confidence and serenity.

Continuation and end of the testimony of Anne Rouchouse (broadcasting manager in the cultural sector)

"I now prepare beforehand as much as possible for potential future speaking, in order to have time to explore and soak up the subject I am dealing with. Assimilating information that is directly or indirectly related to my subject keeps me calm about the moment to come.

I draw up a detailed plan of the speech as I imagine it, then write out everything I will say, then learn it practically off by heart. Of course, the initial framework is retouched several times during the oral adaptation stage. I learn the reworked version by heart.

As someone who memorises information mainly by reading, the process of working on the framework to fit an oral style, proofreading and correcting it in writing helps me a lot to learn it. Therefore, I only need to repeat it a few times afterwards to fully learn it.

I time myself, even if the presentation does not have a time limit. I find it reassuring to master the time factor, although we tend to express ourselves at a different speed to normal speech.

The day before the speech, I practice just before bed, because I really feel it helps to "sleep on it"!

I make sure I have time to repeat my presentation shortly before the fateful time. If all goes well, I trust myself and most of my stress vanishes. If it does not go so well I make note of passages that seem more difficult, in order to better address them at the time of the presentation.

During the presentation, I keep my notes with me in full (not a simple plan). Although, usually, I do not need them, simply knowing that I can find any idea from my presentation if I need to reassures me.

Finally, I always make eye contact in the room as well as

regular sweeping glances to encourage the audience's attention."

TOP 10 TIPS

1. Ask yourself the right questions before jumping into preparing your speech. What kind of audience will you be addressing? What is the purpose of your speech? These questions will effectively guide your preparation and help you save time for your future planning.
2. Do breathing exercises. Before you start, take time to work through some simple breathing exercises. Some theatrical practices are useful to monitor your heart rate and "release negative vibes".
3. Pay particular attention at the beginning of your speech. Getting started well will give you more confidence for the rest. Prepare a hook or an original introduction. A humorous anecdote is often a good way to break the ice.
4. If possible, avoid writing out your entire speech and do not read your notes during the speech. Think spontaneous and natural!
5. Practice as much as possible. The more time you take to go over your speech, the better you will master it and feel at ease when the time comes. Practicing lowers stress substantially.
6. Do not focus your attention on the image you want to portray. Instead, focus on the consistency between your gestures and your speech. It is important that your attitude does not contradict what you say.
7. Be attentive to your audience and show flexibility. You cannot predict audience involvement, but you can correct yourself, provided you are well prepared and comfortable with the subject.

8. Do not allow yourself to be disturbed by external elements. Again, there will always be some unknown elements that you cannot control. However, you can control your reactions and keep smiling, as well as maintain the same dynamism despite the unexpected.

9. Adopt good posture by standing up straight. Although this may seem unimportant, studies have shown that standing well can not only reduce anxiety and stress, but it can also give you more confidence and energy. Furthermore, it can help to improve your breathing, which is especially vital if you are required to speak for over 30 minutes.

10. Do not rely on your visual aids, as they are only tools. If you use a *PowerPoint* presentation, do not overload the slides, simplify them. The goal is to help your audience follow the progression of your speech and retain information in a few keywords. You must remain the main focus of the presentation.

"Speaking in public, that's working". Here are some tips from the observation and practice of public speaking by Georges Peillon (consultant, trainer and assistant in crisis communication).

> 90% of success lies in the preparation of a speech. Without a doubt, if you are called upon to speak, that means you are considered the most able to talk about the subject...so you need to put all the odds on your side.
>
> Very unequal in a speaking situation, some come directly in connection with their audience, while others need to warm up, i.e. with repetitions. Public speaking is a bit like when you sit on a chair: it takes four feet to be stable.

• **The subject.** Are you the best person to speak about this subject? If the answer is no, choosing to step down rather than take the adventure involves risks, mainly in the image you send to others. If, on the other hand, you are the expert, you cannot escape this task. You will therefore need to plan sufficient preparation time to prepare what you will say.

• **The audience.** Who will they be? Will they be familiar with the topic or do you need to popularise it? The answers to these questions are essential if you want to keep the attention of your audience!

• **The context.** Under what conditions are you going to speak? What are the technical requirements? Who will speak before and after you? How much time will you need to speak?

• **The speaker.** How are you feeling? Are you nervous or stressed? If the answer is yes, this will show. Remind yourself of soothing images to monitor the situation and try to decrease your jitters. Do some breathing exercises.

I'll leave you with an anecdote. During a seminar attended by 150 directors of communication, a speaker was to present on economic intelligence. He was one of the best experts in the field, yet his presentation proved to be a disaster for two reasons. First, it was impossible for him to dominate the stage due to the fright that paralysed him: he could only babble and seemed confused. Then, eager to deliver a lot of information, he drowned in the support aids on the screen. He had obviously stayed up the night before, changing his statements by adding and removing information. After his speech, nobody understood the concept of economic intelligence...

In conclusion, you must deliver a simple speech (though not simplistic), because what you say is what matters most. Nothing else.

FAQS

WHY ARE WE AFRAID OF PUBLIC SPEAKING?

Glossophobia, or the fear of public speaking, comes primarily from a fear of judgment and the eyes of others. It may also be rooted in other factors, such as:

- fear of failure
- fear of saying anything
- fear of ridicule
- fear of experiencing a solitary moment
- often, a combination of all these fears.

Detecting what scares you personally can be done by asking yourself the right questions – "Why am I so afraid of speaking in public?" or "What am I risking when speaking in front of others?" – in order to start working on yourself. Once you have identified the sources, you will find it easier to face them.

WHAT PRACTICAL EXERCISES CAN HELP TO OVERCOME STRESS?

Breathing exercises

You can use simple breathing exercises, which will allow you to focus on your heart rate and keep you calm. Breathing in counts of four and breathing while walking, as discussed previously, are quick and simple to do. Other rapid relaxation exercises will allow you to relieve stress:

- **Scanning**, which involves positioning the fingertips of both hands on your forehead at the hairline, then dragging them outwards until they reach the face. Repeating this motion in the same area three times can also be performed on other parts of the face (base of the nose, eyelids, cheeks, mouth, chin, neck).
- **Quick sauna**, by rubbing the hands together vigorously until they heat up, then placing the palms on closed eyes and breathing quietly until the palms cool.
- **Self-massage**, either at the temples, plexus or cheeks.

Furthermore, abdominal breathing, embellished with some gestures, helps to significantly calm you down and regain normal heart rate and body confidence. Proceed as follows:

- Step 1: Relax your muscles, place on hand on your stomach and close your eyes;
- Step 2: Inhale deeply through your nose, making your stomach swell, while performing a massage around your navel;
- Step 3: Exhale slowly through the mouth while continuing to massage around the navel;
- Step 4: Repeat the exercise several times, focusing on breathing in and out into the stomach and the massages designed to relax your abdominal area.

Exercises inherited from the theatre

There are also many exercises practiced in the theatre that allow you to imagine yourself speaking and play out the speech. Although they are more difficult to practice alone, some exercises are still achievable individually:

- Talking as quickly as possible. The aim is to develop imagination and verbal fluency under stress. It is possible, for example, to do this exercise to add slightly more difficulty to your presentation and try to present or explain the points as quickly as possible. This technique will help you to ultimately find faster and simpler ways to explain things and thus perform more calmly on the day;
- Consider every member of the audience instead of the group. If it is the eyes of others that make you anxious, this exercise will gradually help you to overcome this. If you are not able to perform this exercise with a sufficient number of people, you can try it in secret: while walking in the street, try really looking at the people you pass, or stopping at a dead end, as if you were expecting someone, and paying attention to the looks that people give you. For example, you can wear a coloured garment to attract attention and thus be really confronted with the looks of others;
- Imagine realistically what you want to see happen during your presentation. For this to work, it is necessary for the projection/display to be realistic and based on concrete elements. Therefore, you can imagine the end of your presentation and the remarks made by a few people from the audience in discussions. Through this exercise, it is essential that you pay attention to the sensations felt, your state of mind and any associated feelings.

As each person is different, you should seek, test and apply several exercises that will have a real impact on the management of your stress. You can also attend workshops or improvisational acting classes, which will help you work not only on your verbal communication, but also your nonverbal communication and develop some ability to take a step back to analyse the image your project, to determine what will have a real effect on your stress and apprehension. Take control of yourself!

HOW CAN I PREPARE MY SPEECH?

Good preparation requires time and persistence. You must be open to the idea that you will have to recite your speech several times, change aspects and, in short, look at your presentation from all directions until you have completely mastered it.

Overall you should think about:

- asking the right questions from the start;
- looking for information you may be missing;
- making a clear plan to be able to deliver a specific percussive and professional message;
- working on the structure by repeating your speech again and again;
- thinking of a hook that will help you to attract the audience's attention from the beginning.

WHAT MISTAKES SHOULD BE AVOIDED?

There are many pitfalls that you should avoid. Among these errors are:

- neglecting your audience;
- neglecting your presentation;

- playing a role;
- being too serious and distant;
- reading from your *PowerPoint* presentation;
- reading or reciting your notes;
- use language parasites ("uh", "so", "suddenly", etc.);
- remaining frozen.

Do everything you can to grab and hold the attention of your audience!

WHAT SHOULD I DO IF I LOSE TRACK OF MY PRESENTATION?

It is not uncommon to lose track of what you are saying under the effect of hyper-concentration or after an interruption. Don't panic! If this happens, grab your notes to check them with a quick glance. The visual tricks you developed at the beginning will help to regain your spirits and continue calmly with your presentation. For example, think about organising your notes as follows:

- on one side, your written speech;
- on the other side, your speech plan and visual schematic.

HOW CAN I REMAIN CALM WHEN FACED WITH A DIFFICULT QUESTION?

Managing your reactions and keeping your cool are an automation that you need to quickly adopt: they will come through your speaking experiences. In addition to improving the quality of your presentations at work, this will help you in everyday life.

Keep in mind that the audience is not, in principle, there to put you off or make you uncomfortable. Everyone knows the difficulty involved in this type of exercise and if a question you hadn't thought about is asked, don't rush. Take your time to think and respond, because ultimately, it is YOU who is leading the presentation, so enjoy it!

Finally, although you have prepared the content of your presentation, sometimes you're not an expert. Therefore, be bold enough to admit your approximate knowledge of the subject by answering with "I'm not able to answer that yet" or "I don't want to give an inaccurate answer". Besides, if you pretend you know everything about a subject you may come across as pretentious. Don't be afraid, if the situation allows, to take the details of the person and get back to them after doing some additional research.

SHOULD I BE AFRAID OF SILENCE?

Silences can be very destabilising for some people. However, talking quickly and filling every second to compensate for stress and to finish a presentation as soon as possible will certainly cause instant disinterest from your audience. Therefore, adopt behaviour that appears poised, natural and sincere.

Silences are useful for two similar reasons:

- breathing
- slower speech rate.

That said, please do not go the other direction and talk far too slowly or abuse silences. As with everything else, you need to find the right balance! Practicing will help you a lot with this task.

IS A *POWERPOINT* PRESENTATION ALWAYS NECESSARY?

At first glance, everything suggests that the need for a visual medium depends on the topic – what you are going to discuss – and the context – where you deliver your speech. Yet, it has become rather rare for a presentation not to be accompanied by visual aids (usually a *PowerPoint*). In fact, this tool has been gradually imposed and now appears essential for any presentation. It is advised according to the following framework:

- a presentation that lasts more than 20 minutes;
- a complex presentation or one that involves a lot of numbers.

By choosing to present a visual medium including structured and reusable information, you can facilitate the understanding of the people to whom you are speaking. This support will also help you to remember more data as a presentation of more than 20 minutes implies rather dense content.

 For some presentations, including internal meetings, it can be interesting and informative to deliver presentations with no *PowerPoint* support from time to time and build on your speaking skills which are greatly strengthened by the practice. Setting yourself challenges is exactly how you will end up enjoying speaking.

OVER TO YOU

Succeeding in public speaking, persuading or delivering a message is possible for everyone, as it is possible to remove or bypass any potential sources of stress through the implementation of the following tips!

1. Start by targeting the causes of stress.
2. Discover the associated fears.
3. Come up with action plans to improve the situation and get past what is holding you back.

The necessary steps to move forward

Preparing a presentation

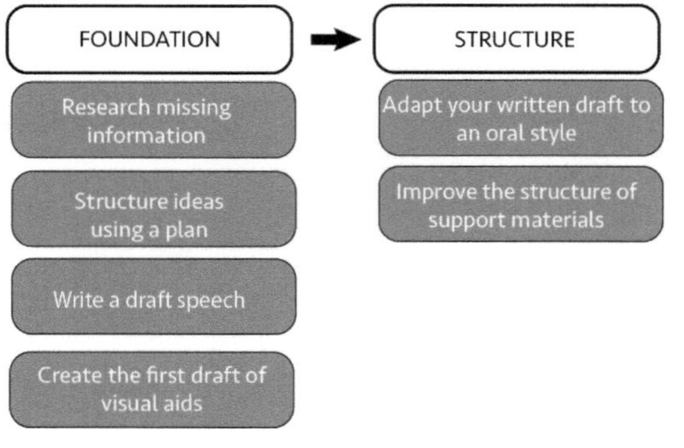

Since everything is a matter of preparation and work, consider what slows you down or gives you trouble and dedicate your time to that. Only you can decide to get out of the spiral, so the rest is up to you!

We want to hear from you!
Leave a comment on your online library
and share your favourite books on social media!

FURTHER READING

BIBLIOGRAPHY

- Franc Desages, C. (2014) Comment gérer la peur de parler en public ? *L'Express.fr.* [Online]. [Accessed 18 July 2016]. Available from: <http://www.lexpress.fr/styles/psycho/glossophobie-commentgerer-la-peur-de-parler-en-public_1537311.html>
- Gannac, A. L. (2002) Parler face au public. *Psychologies.com.* [Online]. [Accessed 18 July 2016]. Available from: <http://www.psychologies.com/Moi/Moi-et-les-autres/Timidite/Articles-et-Dossiers/Oser-se-parler/Parler-face-au-public>
- Grange, P. (2013) *Prise de parole en public à l'usage des managers et des communicants.* Paris: Faits & Chiffres.
- Holmes, L. (2014) Bienfaits d'une bonne posture sur le stress, la productivité…: 6 raisons de bien vous tenir droit. *The Huffington Post.* [Online]. [Accessed 18 July 2016]. Available from: <http://www.huffingtonpost.fr/2014/10/08/bienfaits-posturestress-productivite-tenir-droit_n_5943986.html>
- Rouden, E. (2011) 6 exercices de relaxation contre le stress. *Femina.fr.* [Online]. [Accessed 18 July 2016]. Available from: <http://www.femina.fr/Sante-Forme/Bien-etre/6-exercicesde-relaxation-contre-le-stress>
- Semeunacte, M. (2014) 7 techniques d'orateur efficace (et intéressant… pour changer). *Semeunacte.com.* [Online]. [Accessed 18 July 2016]. Available from: <http://semeunacte.com/orateur-efficace>
- Sorzana, C. (2010) *La prise de parole en public.* Paris:

Victoires Éditions.

50MINUTES.com

IMPROVE YOUR GENERAL KNOWLEDGE

IN A BLINK OF AN EYE !

www.50minutes.com

www.50minutes.com

Ebook EAN: 9782806269690

Paperback EAN: 9782806284013

Legal Deposit: D/2016/12603/347

Cover: © Primento

Digital conception by Primento, the digital partner of publishers.